A WHISPER OF MY HEART

MILLION THOUGHTS

ANIL K ARORA

Dedicated to:

my mother, who is always my support system, and who loves me more than I deserve.

my father, who has done a lot for me without even telling me.

my brother, who is always a blessing for me.

and the one who is in my mind while writing those poetries.

Contents

Contents

Contents

Contents

Acknowledgements

Writing a book is harder than I thought and more rewarding than I could have ever imagined. None of this would have been possible without my best friend, Siddu. She was the first friend I made when I when I started writing something. She encouraged me everytime for my writings. She stood by me during every struggle and all my successes. That is true friendship.

I'm eternally grateful to my Brother, Happy, who took in an extra mouth to feed when he didn't have to. He taught me discipline, tough love, manners, respect, and so much more that has helped me succeed in life.

To my father and my mother, for always encouraging me to do different tasks in life, and always being there with me at my worst.

Foreword

It's truly a joy to write this special foreword to *A Whisper of My Heart*for my beloved readers. This book contains millions of emotions and feelings, I believe that you will definitely feel connected to these emotions. I would like to thank you for picking this book up.

There are many languages in the world but love has only one language. Love should be expressed to your beloved partner for sure. I believe that this book will be your language to express your emotions and feelings to your loved one.

Make sure your loved one is in your mind while reading these writings, this will surely help you to make a soulful connection with the book.

She is a dream

Don't love her like some competition,

then you keep her as your medal,

love her like a dream that you chase every single day.

Fear of Love

If I fall in love again, then I want it to last forever,
no breakups anymore, I am tired of them in the past,

I may be smiling but my eyes are full of tears,
people call them magical words, but they are my fear,

I am hard to love, as cracks in my heart are fresh,
but my soul is fresh, only hard is the flesh,

don't promise me forever, just prove me wrong,
don't leave me stuck, on another sad song.

Tale of love

Me: *Dadi don't come to school,*
my friend is coming to pick me up.
Dadi: *Nai Bache, I am completely fine now,*
I can come to drop you at the school.

They both lied in love and care.

A Short Fantasy

I don't know why but I want to walk barefoot on a black beach with you. Watch the sunset - and - watch your features turn into a beautiful silhouette. As the evening would sink into darkness and we will lay on the beach to watch the stars and crescent moon - I want to smell the salty ocean on your skin. Then I will dive into your mouth with my tongue. I will flow boundlessly into you like a river flows into the ocean. I will swim with you. I will dive into you. I will drown you. Then with my taste on your breath, I want to hear my name from your mouth. I just want you to whisper those magical words in my ear, Yes! those magical words that I will store in some dark corner of my heart, and at the age of 60 when I'll be sitting on a couch and looking into that beautiful evening, I will take those memories out from my heart to keep myself warm.

Cute Romance

After her full-day classes,
she was tired when they met in the park,
He found peace seeing her sleepy face on his shoulder...

Come back

1 Message Received.
"Hi...!"

ab teen saalon baad kyu yaar?
Suddenly he was lost somewhere, in the past memories where he was blindly in love with someone. And he wasn't able to understand why his eyes are showering for no reason.

Cute Romance

He: *"Why don't you date me?"*
She: *Why do you want to date me?*
and What to date with?
a half heart? a half soul? a half me?
He: *Let me be a part of your life,*
Let me help you heal first.
Maybe then you'll be ready to start living a new life.

Vichhar

Vibing on a small chai ki tapri and eating on roadside footstalls hit something different.

Love Romance

Love is not about finding the right person..but creating the right relationship. It's not about how much love you have in the beginning..but how much love you build till the end. A perfect relationship isn't actually perfect at all, it consists of two people who never give up on each other despite any hurt or pain... I don't want to give up on you. I want to make life with you. I am waiting for you. I'll be waiting till every extent.

Fairy Tales

I catch some fireflies and release them on your hair.
The way those luminescent fireflies are dancing upon your hair.
I can bet there's nothing prettiest in the world as you are tonight.

Heart Break

I thought we were sharing that bond with each other where I can feel everything happening in your eyes, but the incoming call from three hearts saved in your phone proved me wrong.

In Love

If you are not in love with her messy morning face every day,
You are not in love enough.

In Love

On this rainy morning, at about 4 AM, half asleep they cuddled each other. Without even realizing their lips just touched each other's and ended up having a wonderful french kiss.

In Love

[illegible] morning, at about 1 A.M., half asleep they cuddled each other [illegible] feeling their lips just touched each others and ended up having [illegible] wonderful [illegible].

In Love

On a rainy morning, as you wake up with your cutest sleepy face in my arms, I find your eyes the prettiest.

In Love

There is definitely some connection between waking up with your dream and smiling all day long.

Yes, I am smiling because I saw us together in my dreams, Love is beautiful. It leaves you breathless. It makes you do silly things. It gives you goosebumps. It changes you forever. Love is hope. It reflects goodness and warmth. Love is finding the right one at the right time. Forget for once about all the pain and negativity. Do not give up. Believe in love. Oh, darling, trust me, the right one will hear your heartbeat...?

Motivation

Your story is written by God! Don't compare it what you have seen in the movies,
Trust me God's plan is definitely better than those scriptwriters.

One of the most dangerous things we can do is to compare our love life with Bollywood movies, where there is always a happy ending and the hero gets a girl of his choice by saving her from the villain. These stories are written by scriptwriters, the only thing in their mind is to make movies more entertaining so that more business can be done.

But your love story is written by God. Here every that happens to you have definitely something meaningful. Stop comparing your love life to these movies things. Just keep loving your partner and be loyal to them. Things will be fine in the end.

Love

Maybe he is not the best at being loved,
but he is pretty amazing at loving.

It may sound toxic but he isn't the easiest person to love, He has his bad habit of overthinking when things are not clear to him, he tends to overreact more than he should, and he gets a little insecure every once in a while. He isn't capable of fully trusting you as you never let him do that. He doesn't know when to stop fighting with you even if he's wrong, because you never let him say whatever he feels like, and he has no problem pushing you away if he feels like you are close to hurting him. He'll be needy for your attention, he'll want to literally take up all of your time, and he'll require a lot of reassurance. Loving him means you get to see him at his worst and most vulnerable and that is something that you'll have to be strong enough to handle because he needs someone who's patient enough to understand why he is, who he is today. It's not gonna be an easy relationship with him. But if he is in love with you, then he can promise that you'll be loved with such passion and intensity that you'll forget what left felt like before he came along because he'll always be there to put your heart back together after breaking it.

Cute Moment

The moment you look into my eyes and my eyes are already looking at you, you may feel a little discomfort but my safe zone belongs to you.

Cute Moment

After his tiring day from the office, He came to her and started sharing his day at a pace of 100 words per minute,

Shhhh! She sealed his mouth with his palm and kissed his cheek.

Love

If you want to last forever, don't rush,
His lips applied tortoise rule on her neck.

Cute Moment

Can I look into your eyes,

because they are saying your words are not able to say.

Love Tale

Come to my dreams sometimes,

You'll see a tale there, about which you have heard in your childhood.

Desire

Sometimes I feel like her wavy hair
crave for my fingers to play with them.

Cute Moment

"Can I get a hug"
She asked just by looking straight into my eyes and rubbing her palm on my beard.

Magical Tale

"I feel like I am in love with you,"

nudging his beard with her fingertips, she confesses.

"How often did you feel it?" He asks, grabbing her close.

"24th time, today, she tells,

"infinity times, since we met."

Hope

It doesn't have to be bad just because it ended,

Shooting stars are the proof that an ending can also be beautiful.

Moment

While kissing, it was a crazy, sweet tortoise for him

when her palm made its way inside his partly opened shirt.

Still same

Why did you change so much when I am still pure still sweet,

I still smile at the children walking on the street,

I still pause to admire, the flower and the skies,

I still feel the pain when I see you crying,

I still ask my mom to sit by my side when I am sick,

I still finish the Maggi, and then its plate I lick,

I still hide in the blanket, when my heart is broken,

I still feel guilty, that yesterday rudely I had spoken,

Why did you leave me when I am still waiting,

Nothing is on my bucket list until you are not participating.

Still same

Why did you choose to return when I [illegible] with your still [illegible]

I still walk [illegible] of the street.

I still prefer to explore the [illegible] and the stars.

[illegible] when I [illegible] empty.

I still ask [illegible] first.

[illegible] still [illegible] and [illegible] place I [illegible]

I [illegible] when I [illegible]

[illegible]

[illegible]

[illegible]

Scrawled Tale

From, talking for hours,

without realizing, the call duration,

To,

hesitating to dial their number.

Those endless late-night calls slowly turned into empty promises.

Scrawled Tale

Sewn, [illegible] by hours

[illegible] realize [illegible] the real ambition.

[illegible] thoughts of there [illegible]

There [illegible] grew slowly crossed into empty promises.

Pride

His heartfelt pride,

when she introduced him as her man

in a group of friends.

Pride

His heartfelt pride,

when she introduced him as her man

in a group of friends.

Moment

Should I walk to chase you?
Or should I leave you not disturbed?

Should I think of you when I get up?
Or should I leave everything that's related to you?

I am a fairy tale kinda lover,
Should I include you in my story?
Or should I make you a lesson to move on?

Endless Journey

I discover sight

Finding more in you to love

Night by naked night

Music comes to me

In the rhythm of your love

Ballads flowing free

Pleasure is my sea

Your body is my sailboat

Endless this journey...

Nazar na lage

You must put kaala teeka everytime you post a picture, people have nazar on you , including me...

You and I, mountain view from the window in the moonlight night.

Half-burnt cigarette and a glass full of wine.

Lovemaking and raw passion. How about this kinda night?

Her quirky smile when she gets food,

How she dances when she thinks

no one is watching,

Her voice when she calls me and says oeeeo,

All the little things that remind me,

Why she holds a special place in my heart.

She was air, I was fire,

I wanted her to burn a little brighter,

I needed her to need me too,

But she was free,

She belonged to no one...

She was air, I was fire,

I wanted her to burn a little brighter,

I wanted to grab her in my eyes,

I needed her to need me too,

But she was free,

She belonged to no one...

When he writes

She is reflected on each word.

Take your life as a rehearsal for any performance where mistakes are permitted, experimentation is expected, and spontaneity is allowed.

Manzilon ka to kuchhh nahi keh sakta,

par haan mene apni zindgi ka kaafi waqt,

bemaksad ek safar me guzaara hai...

Likh kar apni shayari me tujhe,

kuchhh kaid kar dun is tarah,

ki tu ude bhi toh,

bas ek nazam se dusre nazam tak.

Kuchh khaas umeedien nahi zindagi se magar,

ek aam si zindagi bhaati kise hai.

dhundte dhundte apni zindagi ka maksad,

yun zindagi guzarni kise hai.

mujhe zindagi se shikayat thi ki mujhe mohabbat nahi mili,

maa ne do rotiya ghee lga ke paros di, meri saari shikayatein dur ho gyi.

Dear weekend,

eventually, everyone will move on,

even after you give them hundreds of memories,

but trust me,

everyone will wait for you

to come again.

I love writing your name on paper,
With my ink, letting it dry,
And make an impression

Touching every letter,
And caressing the curves,
Taking my time
To absorb the feeling of your presence

And then
Erase it again to hide you
From the world and keeping you safe
Only in my heart and my mind.

Can I sleep for a while?
And just hope
That it's a nightmare.

Can I just sleep for a while?
And when I wake up
Everything will be alright again.

Can I just sleep for a while?
And hope that
I will open my eyes to a
Good day.

Can I just
Sleep Peacefully
For one night.

Can I just ?

"Jhalla Kahin ka", she used to call her every day,

she never knew how fidelity changed her childhood friend

into a mad lover.

Thelma [illegible], she used to call her every day,

she never knew how quickly changed her [illegible] friend

into a mere letter

People with beautiful hearts,

stay beautiful,

It's people with external beauty

who come with an expiry date.

Lost and Found

I hope one day you find peace within you,
I hope one day you find yourself within you.

From all the wonderful things people can do with their tongues, it's a pity they choose to spew hateful words.

Summer is a season of love. If you will fall in love with yourself only.

Heart Talk

She carries a million broken pieces inside her,

You need to kiss her a million times for her to trust you,

Give her that patience, Give her that loyalty,

and then watch her bloom in love.

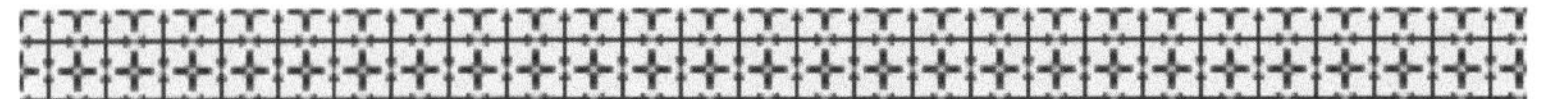

Thode kisse tere ho thodi ho meri kahaani,
majnoo sa me aashiq banu, tu meera si deewani,
aadhi dhoop thoda paani,
ankho me hi baatein ho, ho dilo ki manmaani,
ese hi kat jaaye
teri meri zindgaani...

In the era of "we don't talk anymore like we use to do"

be someone's "Jaane kyu ye dil jaanta hai, tu hai to I'll be alright"

Har ilzaam ko khud se lapet liya tha maine..
badnaami ko apni taraf mod liya tha maine..
Ek khilauna tootne par ro jaya karti thi jo...
ab dil tootne par bhi muskura deti hai..
Ye ishq tha, ya kiya koi sauda tha?
tum ne to yun iss dil ko massal dia..
jaise koi paudha tha.

आसमान के साये में
और पर्वत की बाहों में
मैं हर शाम डूबना चाहता हूं
सिर्फ तेरी ही निगाहों में

Scars

Admire her, not for her smile

not even for her eyes.

Admire her, for the battle scars and wounds that she displays proudly for the world to see.

Ask yourself that ain't the scars beautiful?

ये दो पल की जो जिंदगी है
इसे एक खूबसूरत ख्वाब की तरह
जीना सीखो।
बहुत मुश्किल सा है ये दौर
किसी का सहारा तो किसी की
बेवजह मुस्कुराहट बनना सीखो।

You and I fell in love like a wild flower in the rain♥?
Knowing that you are around.
I've found a reason to love you each second.
I've found it in smallest of the places, majestic vibes.
Making me realize that you are my only paradise.
Yearned for you like a wild child with stain.
Yes! You and I fell in love like a wild flower in the rain.

Ek shaks se yun mulakaat ho gyi
jaise sitaaro bhari koi raat ho gyi

Choo gya hai vo dil ko iss kadar
maano, aaj meri khud se hi mulakaat ho gyi..

wqat ke panne palat kar fir se wo haseen lamhe jeene ko dil chahta hai,

kabhi hasa karte the sab dost milkar, aaj unhe sath dekhne ko dil taras jata hai.

बर्फ़ सी ठण्डी तुम
मैं चाय सा गर्म

तुम चांद सफेद सा
मैं दाग सा कोई रंग

wo bhi tujhe hi sambhalne me kharch ho gya,

mene jo waqt nikaala tha khudke pair jamaane ke liye

बदल देता है चादं भी अपनी जगह
उसकी एक मुस्कुराहट ही इतनी प्यारी है
देखि जाती है वो
रंग और नूर से रंगीन कायनात सारी है

बर्फ़ सी सफ़ेद है वो ठोडी पर तिल विराजमान हैं उनके

मैं रेत सा मटमैला मेरे लिए पैर ही दीवान है उनके

चप्पल से भी नीचे रहता हूँ
मैं बर्फ़ थोडी हूँ जो हर पैमाने में होता हूँ❤?

ऐ हवा जाके कह कर आ उन पहाडी झरनों वाली से

कि तेरे एक बूँद का प्यासा रेगिस्तान में भी इंतज़ार में है

And do understand the fact, you and I are a Universe apart.

You are light.

I am darkness.

They don't go together.

ये दो पल की जो जिंदगी है

इसे एक खूबसूरत ख्वाब की तरह जीना सीखो

बहुत मुश्किल सा है ये दौर

किसी का सहारा तो किसी की बेवजह मुस्कुराहट बनना सीखो

His every smile, his every touch
will remind me of how closely we had
to draw an impossible conclusion.
It breaks me down that we couldn't
make the parallel lines meet.
Forever it was meant to be but
you had someone else's promises to keep.
You broke my heart, you killed my dreams
but I promise to keep loving you
in another time, a different universe,
some other existence, with an invisible connection.

Hearts were [illegible] for every [illegible]
still remind me of your closely the bird
to dream of a possible continued
it breaks me when I see that we could
make the parallel lines meet.
I [illegible] to be [illegible]
you laid on me the promises to each
You broke my heart, you stolen my [illegible]
and promise to keep loving you
in another time, a different universe
[illegible]

Yad hai mujhe vo beeta waqt jab
Sunke jhankaar tere payal ki
laga tha jaise ho gya har raag kaamil
Yad hai mujhe vo teri choodiyo ki khan khan
Sun kar bas behak gya tha mera mann

याद है मुझे वो बीता वक़्त जब
सुनके झनकार तेरे पायल की
लगा था जैसे हो गया हर राग कामिल
याद है मुझे वो तेरी चूड़ियों की खन खन
सुनकर बस बेहक गया था मेरा मन!

Tujhe sawalo mei uljha kar
jee bhar ke dekhna chahta hu
Teri masoomiyat ko apni ankho
mei kaid karna chahta hu
Ye nazrein sirf tujhpe aa kar rukti hain
main sirf tujhe hi apni zindgi ka kaqdaar bnana chahta hu.

तुझे सवालों में उलझा कर
जी भर के देखना चाहता हूं
तेरी मासूमियत को अपनी आंखो
में कैद करना चाहता हूं
ये नज़रें सिर्फ़ तुझपे आकर रुकती हैं
मैं सिर्फ़ तुझे ही अपनी ज़िंदगी का
हकदार बनाना चाहता हूं

un haseen vaadiyon mn
sadak k kinaare khade tu aur main
chai ki chuskiyan lete
ik dooje ki aankhon mn khoye tu aur main
tune apni chai ka gilaas mere haathon mn thamaya
apni zulfon ko thoda suljhaya
aur maine chup chap teri chai vala gilaas apne labon se lgakar
apna gilaas tujhe thamaya
Tujhe is baat ka pta bhi lag gya
aur bavjood uske tune fir vo gilaas apne labon se lgaya
us lamhe mn mera sab kuch reh gya
aur waqt vahin tham gya
tune halke se itrakar is qadar apna dupatta smbhala
is qadar apna dupatta theek kiya
nazren jhukakar, thoda sharmakar
dheeme se muskurakar tune mere gaalon ko hath lgaya
Aur ek hi pal mn tune mujhse mujhi ko chheen liya

Main aaj bhi tere ishq ka izhaar kitaabon mein mehfooz rakhti hoon
Main aaj bhi tere hone ka ehsaas apne gaalon pe mehsoos karti hoon
Main apni zulfon ko is qadar baandh kar rakhti hoon ki kahin chhip na jaaye
vo daayin taraf ka jhumka mera
Aur ek khyaal sa hai ki ek din kho na du tujhe,
main har pal ae mehboob darti hun

Maine bhagwan ko to nahi dekha
lekin, papa ke roop mei unhe dekha hai.
Meri har zarurat puri karne ke liye, maine papa ko hazaar qurbaaniya dete huye dekha hai
Laadli hu na mai papa aap ki?
Maine ye sawaal har dfa unse poocha hai.
Mujhe zra si chot lagne par, pareshan ho uthte ho aap..
Sher bacha hai tu mera!! ye keh kar mujh mein josh bhar dete ho aap...
Ek cheez maangne par, sau cheeze saamne la kar rakh dete ho aap
Papa, bhagwan ka diya hua sab se anmol tohfa ho aap
Mera guroor mera abhimaan ho aap.
Meri duniya or meri har ek saans ho aap
Jaan se badh kar agar koi mera khyaal rakh skta hai to vo ho aap
Maa kahani sunaya karti thi jo, usi kahani wale sapno ke rajkumar ho aap
Log jis superman ki baat karte hai, mere vo Superman ho aap..

Do you still remember his favourite colour?

Yes! right?

Spill your heart out.

Let him know your world still revolves around him

Let him know the beautiful memories will never fade away

Let him know his existence matters

Let him know you are probably still in love with him

Near or far the distance matter matter

Just like a boomerang, true love has a habit of always returning back to you

(Appreciate your beloved ones)

Kya pata kab waqt badal jaaye or unhe nazarandaaz karna ek sabak sikha jaye

When you love someone,
all you want is to spend your whole life with them.
Dear you, I dream of nothing different.

Love is an eternal feeling,
It has no reason and no season.
Dear you,love me for the same feeling
Of eternity.
Because of you,my life
seems so vibrant and new.

Not at any cost I'll let you drift away...
I'm sorry,I'm not perfect
but dear you, I swear I'll love you with all
my imperfections too.

As I woke up in the middle of the
night,with innumerable thoughts of you.
Reminding me of the winters,
When we were close.

Tears were gushing down my cheeks..
When I found you weren't there next to me.
Dear you I was longing for you,
craving for your touch and every moment that we had spent together.

For a second,I forgot where I was,
I opened my eyes,the darkness was
surrounding me and the only thing
that crossed my mind was you.

Dear you, my feeling for you could define
what forever is.
I am only afraid of you walking away
and forgetting me.

I thank heaven for you noticed me,
the only man who added a meaning
to my name.
I love you like no one ever can,
for your touch is like a magic wand.

A true relationship goes through hell but a strong relationship gets through it❣?
There are thick and thins, its all about how do you handle the toughest situations and never ever give up.
What's meant to be, will always be.

I believe that some chirping angels choose fur instead of wings

A dog's paw will always comfort you more than a human hand

they've got different bodies but the same soul!

All good things are wild and free so be kind to everything that lives

Printed by Libri Plureos GmbH in Hamburg,
Germany